NATURE WATCH
CAMELS

Written by
Cherie Winner

Lerner Publications Company • Minneapolis

Lerner Publications Company
A division of Lerner Publishing Group, Inc.
241 First Avenue North
Minneapolis, MN 55401

Website address: www.lernerbooks.com

Library of Congress Cataloging-in-Publication Data

Winner, Cherie.
   Camels / by Cherie Winner.
      p.   cm. — (Nature watch)
   Includes bibliographical references and index.
   ISBN-13: 978–1–57505–870–2 (lib. bdg. : alk. paper)
   1. Camels—Juvenile literature. I. Title.
   QL737.U54W56 2008
   599.63'62—dc22   2007001947

Manufactured in the United States of America
1 2 3 4 5 6 – DP – 13 12 11 10 09 08

CONTENTS

When camels drink, they stretch their long necks down to reach the water.

MASTER OF THE DESERT

ON A HOT MORNING, FIVE CAMELS PICK THEIR WAY ALONG A rocky trail. Ahead lies a cool pond surrounded by tall bushes. The camels have been walking for 5 days without a drink. When the pond comes into view, the camels pause and sniff the air. The area is empty of people. The camels are safe. They step to the edge of the pond, lower their heads, and drink.

For thousands of years, people have marveled at how camels can travel for days under the blazing sun without eating or drinking. People have relied on camels to help them cross **deserts**. People have laughed at camels' long faces and funny expressions and told folktales about them. And people have wondered about their humps.

Left: Dromedaries have one hump.
Below: Bactrian camels have two humps.

> To remember the difference between dromedaries and Bactrian camels, think of the letters *D* and *B* lying on their sides. The *D*, for dromedary, has one "hump," while the *B*, for Bactrian, has two.

There are two **species**, or kinds, of camels. Those with one hump are called Arabian camels, or **dromedaries** (DRAH-mah-dair-ees). Their scientific name is *Camelus dromedarius*. The name *dromedary* comes from a Greek word that means "runner." Dromedaries are native to the deserts of northern Africa and the Middle East. Camels with two humps are called **Bactrian** (BAK-tree-uhn) **camels.** *Camelus bactrianus* is their scientific name. Bactrian camels are native to western and central Asia. They were named for Bactria, an ancient country that existed where modern-day Afghanistan, Uzbekistan, and Tajikistan meet.

A camel's **habitat**, or natural territory, is the desert. Deserts are usually hot and dry. But the ancestors of camels did not live in deserts. From about two million years ago to a few thousand years ago, they lived on the grassy prairies of North America. They roamed hundreds of miles every year in search of food and water.

When camels lived in North America, Earth went through several ice ages. During the ice ages, Earth was very cold. Glaciers, or vast sheets of ice, covered many northern lands. Much of the water on Earth was frozen into ice, so the oceans were much lower than they are in modern times. Some areas that are covered by water in modern times were dry land back then.

One of these areas linked North America with Asia. It is known as the Bering land bridge. The word *bridge* makes it sound like a narrow strip of land with waves lapping at both sides. But the Bering land bridge did not look like a bridge. It was hundreds of miles wide.

Camels are better suited to desert life than other kinds of animals.

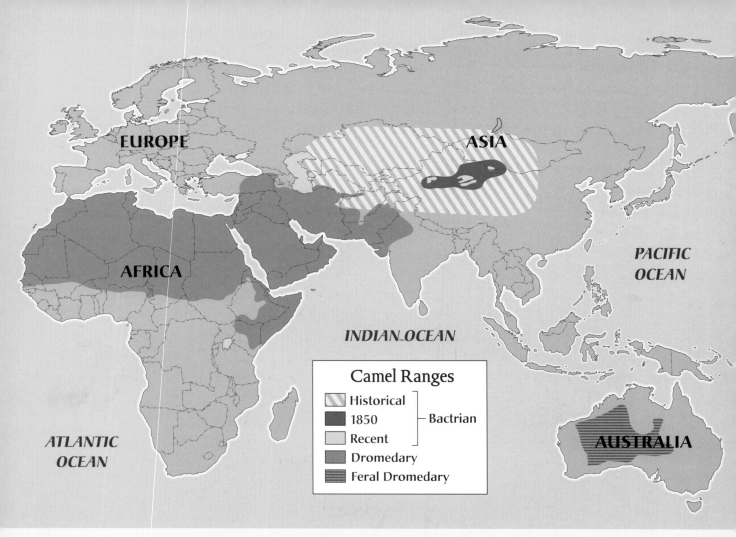

EUROPE

ASIA

PACIFIC OCEAN

AFRICA

INDIAN OCEAN

ATLANTIC OCEAN

AUSTRALIA

Camel Ranges

Historical ⎫
1850 ⎬ Bactrian
Recent ⎭
Dromedary
Feral Dromedary

This map shows how the Bactrian camels' range has shrunk, from ancient times to 1850 to modern times. It also shows the current range of dromedaries.

Scientists believe that many species of animals traveled over the Bering land bridge. Some animals, such as humans, moved from Asia into North America. Primitive camels went the other direction, walking from North America to Asia. Some made their homes in the hilly deserts of Asia. Their descendants, or offspring of many generations, became two-humped Bactrian camels. Others walked all the way to the Middle East and northern Africa. Their descendants became one-humped dromedaries.

About 11,000 years ago, the last ice age ended. Glaciers melted, the oceans rose, and the Bering land bridge disappeared underwater. Early camels that still lived in North America had to stay there. Over the next 2,000 years, they all died out, perhaps because of hunting by humans. Meanwhile, the camels in Asia and Africa thrived in their new homes. They also attracted attention from humans.

At first, people in Asia and Africa hunted wild camels for meat, just as people in North America did. Later, in about 2500 B.C., people captured and **domesticated** (duh-MEH-stih-kay-tid) camels. Domesticated animals have been adapted for human use. After camels were domesticated, people drank camels' milk. They used camels' wool to make clothing, blankets, and tents. They used camels' skin to make leather. Camels also carried heavy loads over rocky mountain trails and endless desert sands. Camels made it possible for people to live in barren lands where cattle, pigs, and other domesticated animals could barely survive.

While domesticated camels thrived, wild camels struggled. Wild dromedaries became **extinct**, or died out, at least 2,000 years ago. No one knows exactly why. In modern times, all the dromedaries in the world are domesticated.

Beginning about 150 years ago, European settlers brought domesticated dromedaries to Australia. Some of the camels escaped. Their descendants live in the Outback, a vast, mostly desert area with few people. Although these camels live in the wilderness, they are not wild camels. They are called **feral**— a name for domesticated animals living on their own, without people.

Most Bactrian camels are domesticated too. They provide wool, milk, meat, and transportation for people living off the land in central Asia. The only wild camels alive in modern times are Bactrian camels living in the deserts of Mongolia and China.

People have depended on camels for food, clothing, and transportation for almost 5,000 years.

An Odd-Looking Creature

Camels are mammals—animals that have hair and that nurse their young. They belong to the camel family, or **Camelidae** (kuh-MEL-ih-dee). Camels are closely related to vicuñas (vy-KOO-nyuhs) and guanacos (gwuh-NAH-kohs). These wild animals live in the mountains of South America. When vicuñas and guanacos were domesticated, they developed into new species. Guanacos became animals called llamas. Vicuñas became alpacas. All these animals, along with camels, belong to the camel family. They are called **camelids**.

All camelids have long legs and long necks. All are suited for life in dry climates. But only camels have humps. Nobody knows why Bactrian camels have two humps and drome-daries have only one. Camels' humps are made of fat and body tissue. They feel firm to the touch, like the base of your ears. They do not contain bones.

Llamas *(below)* and alpacas *(right)* are raised all over the world for their fine wool. Llamas and alpacas resemble camels, but they are smaller, have more hair, and do not have humps.

A camel's hair protects it from the sun. This close-up view shows the long guard hairs on a Bactrian camel's humps.

Both dromedaries and Bactrian camels stand 6 to 7 feet (1.8–2.1 m) tall at the shoulder. Their humps can reach more than 2 feet (0.6 m) higher than that. In both species, males are larger than females. Bactrian camels weigh between 1,000 and 1,400 pounds (454–635 kg). Dromedaries grow to be different sizes. Slender racing camels weigh just 660 pounds (300 kg). Sturdy pack animals can weigh up to 1,500 pounds (680 kg).

Camels have large eyes and long faces with small ears.

Camels can be dark brown, tan, beige, or nearly white, although dromedaries tend to be lighter in color than Bactrian camels. Both species have an undercoat of soft, woolly hair close to the skin. They also have outer coats of long, coarse guard hairs that protect the camel from thorns and blowing sand. The guard hairs are longest on their heads, necks, legs, and humps.

Camels have large, dark brown eyes and small ears that point straight up, like a horse's ears. Their long faces and bumpy foreheads give them comical expressions. They have long necks that dip toward the ground and then rise straight up, so their heads sit at about the same height as their humps. At their back ends, camels have narrow waists and slender tails with long hairs at the tips.

Camels come in several different colors. Dromedaries are usually lighter in color, ranging from white *(left)* to a darker tan *(bottom)*. Bactrian camels can be many shades of brown *(below)*.

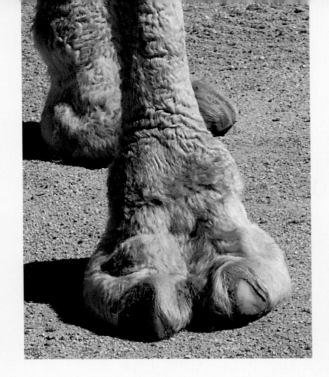

All camels have long legs and unusual feet. Instead of a hoof, each foot has two toes, complete with toenails. The bottom of each foot is covered with loose, leathery skin. This skin lets the toes spread apart when the camel walks, so it doesn't sink far into the sand.

Camels are very intelligent. They recognize names that people give them. If treated with kindness, they are affectionate with their human handlers. Even after several generations in the wild, feral dromedaries will accept human company. After a few days, ranchers can handle them with ease.

Above: Camels' feet are designed for walking through the hot sand.
Below: An owner talks to a camel at a camel festival in India. The festival features camel races and other special events.

This Bactrian camel shows off its mouthful of teeth.

Camels are **herbivores**, or plant eaters. Their mouths are made for eating desert plants. Their tongues and cheeks are tough enough to handle thorns and prickly leaves. A camel's upper lip is split in the middle. Each side—either the left or the right—can grasp a twig or a bunch of leaves and pull it into the mouth. A camel nips off a bite of food by pressing it between sharp teeth on its lower jaw and hard, toothless gums at the front of its upper jaw. Then large teeth in the back of the mouth grind the food before swallowing.

Camels look strange, but they can travel long distances, withstand intense heat, and eat almost any plant. They are perfectly suited for life in the desert.

At Home
in the Desert

ALL CAMELS LIVE IN DESERTS, AND ALL DESERTS ARE DRY.
But not all deserts are the same. Deserts may have sandy or rocky
ground. They may be flat or hilly. They may have many plants or almost
no plants. Deserts also have different kinds of weather.

Dromedaries live in the hottest deserts, where summer lasts five to six
months. Summer temperatures there can reach 140°F (60°C). These
deserts also have short, cold winters. Bactrian camels live in colder
deserts. Summers there are hot but last only two or three months.
During winter, temperatures may drop to –40°F (–40°C). Bactrian
camels have stockier bodies and thicker coats than dromedaries. These
traits help Bactrian camels stay warm during harsh winters.

Both dromedaries and Bactrian camels have special features that help them survive the desert heat. A camel's dense fur protects it from sunburn. Above each eye, two rows of long eyelashes shade the eyes from sunlight. When the wind whips up, a camel can close its nostrils to keep sand out of its nose. Bushy hairs keep sand out of its ears.

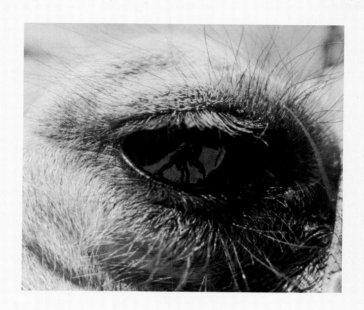

Right: Two rows of top eyelashes offer extra protection from the sun's glare.

Bactrian camels live in colder deserts. Their thick coats help them survive the cold winter months.

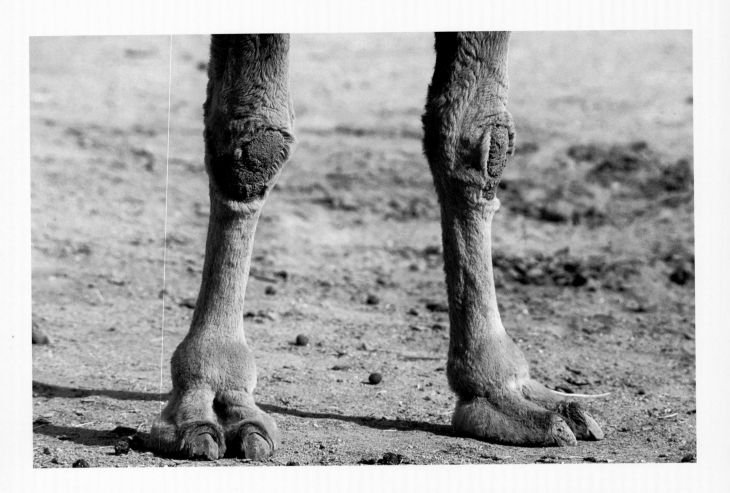

While the sun blazes overhead, camels also get scorched from below. That's because desert sands can heat up to 176°F (80°C) in summer. Camels' long legs lift them high enough to let cooler air flow under their bellies. The bottoms of their feet have leathery pads that don't burn easily. And when camels settle onto the ground for a rest, thick patches of skin called **calluses** protect their knees, elbows, and chests from the roasting-hot sand.

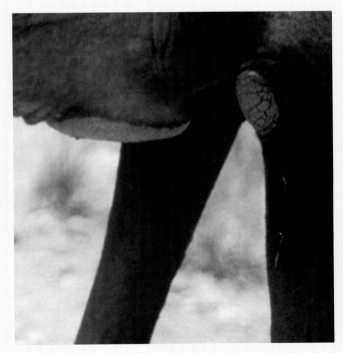

Camels develop calluses on their knees *(above)*, elbows, and chests *(right)* at about 2 months of age.

Camels are most active early and late in the day, when temperatures are cooler. They rest during the hottest midday hours. When they rest, they lie down with all four legs folded under them. This position protects their legs from the sun. They also bunch up together, because lying next to another camel is cooler than being surrounded by the roasting air.

When it is very hot, a camel's body temperature might rise to 106°F (41°C) during the daytime. At night, when temperatures fall, the extra heat built up during the day spreads out into the cooler air. The camel's temperature falls to 93°F (34°C). In the morning, the camel is ready to start a new day under the desert sun. If a person got that hot and then that cool, he or she might die. But this change in temperature doesn't sicken camels at all.

By tucking their legs underneath them and huddling together in groups, camels keep warm in winter as well as cool in summer. If camels stay in one spot during the day, they will turn to keep their heads pointing toward the sun. That keeps them cooler than letting the sun shine on their broad sides.

This camel lives at a zoo in Illinois. One of its humps has fallen over to one side. After the camel eats well, the hump will fill with fat.

All mammals, including people, need water to drink and to help them keep cool. But the deserts where camels live get only 2 to 6 inches (5–15 cm) of rain a year. Unlike many animals, camels can survive in this dry environment.

Most mammals sweat when they get hot. As the sweat evaporates, or dries up, the skin cools down. If camels have plenty to drink, they sweat and stay cool too. But if they don't have enough to drink, they don't sweat much. They just let themselves get hot.

When camels have plenty to drink, they release extra water in their urine and feces. When camels don't have enough to drink, their bodies conserve, or save, water. Their urine becomes brown and thick, like pancake syrup. Their dung comes out as dry pellets. They are so dry that people can use them to fuel campfires.

Camels' humps also help them survive in the desert. People once thought that camels carried water in their humps. But that's not true. Camel humps are filled with fat. The humps get bigger when

You can tell if camels have been burning the fat in their humps for energy. If a dromedary has been burning its fat, its hump will shrink. If a Bactrian camel has been burning its fat, its humps will get wobbly and flop over to one side, like empty sacks. When the camels eat well again, their humps will fill up with more fat.

camels eat a lot. They shrink when camels go hungry. Most mammals have a layer of fat under their skin, all over the body. For camels and other desert animals, having fat all over the body would make them too hot. They stay cooler by having the fat all in one place, in the hump.

Camels use the fat in their humps as a backup fuel supply. When they can't find enough food, they use the fat for energy. On long treks through their barren homelands, camels often go hungry. The fat in their humps lets them keep moving.

ON THE MOVE

IN THE DESERTS WHERE CAMELS LIVE, SOURCES OF FOOD and water are often many miles apart. Water is especially hard to find. The deserts where camels live have few rivers and lakes. They get only a few inches of rain each year. Many months might pass without any rain at all.

Camels are well suited to this dry environment. They can go without eating or drinking for amazing lengths of time. In winter, when it's cold outside, they don't need to sweat to stay cool. So they don't need much water. They may not drink for months in winter. They get all the water they need in their food. In summer, a camel that is working hard can go 2 or 3 days without drinking. A camel that is not working hard can go 8 days or even longer without taking a drink.

The main sources of water in deserts are **oases** (oh-AY-sees). Oases are green areas in the desert. An oasis forms where underground water sits close beneath the ground. Plant roots reach down to the water. Trees and shrubs thrive at oases. They provide shade and water for travelers of many species. At some oases, water flows all the way to the surface and forms a pond. At other oases, people dig wells to reach the water. They lift it out with buckets or pumps so that they and their animals can drink.

Oases are usually 25 to 30 miles (40–48 km) apart—a 2-day walk for a healthy camel. If camels find plenty of food along the trail, the trip between oases isn't hard. But in some places, oases are 50 to 60 miles (80–97 km) away from one another, with no food along the trail. Then camels must walk for many days to find food and water. That's when their ability to stay cool and survive without eating and drinking saves the day.

Top: Camels graze for 8 to 12 hours every day.
Above: This is a trail left by camels as they traveled through the desert.

23

Some oases have existed for centuries. Others last just a few years or have water for only a few months each year. When an oasis disappears, camels and other wildlife must find other sources of water.

When camels finally reach an oasis after a long trek, the first thing they do is drink. A camel can drink up to 8 gallons (30 liters) of water in a minute, but usually it drinks more slowly. Sometimes, one long drink is enough. Other times, the camel drinks and then takes a break. It eats a bit and rests for a few hours. Then it takes another big drink. A biologist once measured how much water camels drank. One male dromedary drank 26 gallons (98 liters) in less than 15 minutes and drank 25 gallons (95 liters) more later the same day.

Most of the time, camels stay at an oasis for just a day or two. Then they head out to find food. If they stayed at one oasis too long, they would soon strip the plants of their leaves, take too much water from the pond, and trample the ground into a muddy mess. By roaming, camels get the food and water they need without harming the oases they depend on.

On the journey between oases, camels graze on the plants they find along the way. Camels are not picky eaters. They devour thorns, spiny leaves, and salty plants that would make most other animals sick.

Camels have stomachs with three chambers. They chew their food several times before it is fully digested. Food first goes into the largest chamber. There, tiny organisms called bacteria start to break down the food. Then the camel vomits up a **cud**, a wad of partly digested food from the first chamber. The camel chews the cud to grind the food even more. Then it swallows the food again and brings up another cud. Eventually, the food is mushy enough to move into the next

When camels smell rain in the distance, they hurry toward it. If they get there soon enough, they might find rainwater pooled at the base of a hill or running in small streams. But in the desert, the water will usually dry up within days.

two chambers of the stomach, where digestion is completed.

Camels graze vegetation on the ground, as well as use their long necks to reach leaves on trees.

FAMILY LIFE

DURING MOST OF THE YEAR, BULLS (MALE CAMELS) AND cows (female camels) live apart. Bulls travel alone or in small herds of 3 to 15 individuals. Cows and their young travel in groups that come together, drift apart, and come together again, depending on how much food they find. Several dozen camels might graze together at a lush oasis and then split into groups of 2 or 3 when they reach drier ground.

Bulls and cows come together when the breeding season begins. Usually this is in winter, but in some places, it occurs during a summer rainy season. When a bull is ready to mate, he tries to gather cows into a **harem**, or breeding herd. He goes into a condition called **musth**. During this time, he paces, roars, and foams at the mouth. Two glands on the back of his head make a smelly oil that attracts cows. The bull bends his neck back and rubs the oil on the front of his hump, where cows can sniff it more easily. His urine also attracts females.

He uses it like perfume. He urinates on his own tail and then slaps himself with his tail to spread the urine around.

A bull in musth is very aggressive. If he already has a harem, he fights to keep other bulls away. If he doesn't yet have a harem, he tries to steal cows from another male. Two bulls might fight over a harem. When they fight, they bellow and bump each other. If one doesn't back down, they fight harder. They try to push each other to the ground with their necks. They slash at each other with their sharp teeth. Sometimes a camel bites so deeply that his opponent bleeds to death. Other times, bulls twist their necks together, causing both to stop breathing. Some bulls die, but usually, both survive the fight.

Male camels twist their necks together as they fight over a harem.

A pregnant Bactrian camel

The loser must look for females elsewhere. He may not mate at all that year. The winner gets to keep the harem, which may include 20 or more females. Some females in the harem are already pregnant from mating the year before. They do not mate with the bull. The others mate with the bull as the harem travels through the desert. After several weeks, the bull gets tired and leaves. He joins a group of other males or wanders alone. The harem then breaks up into smaller groups.

Camels usually give birth to just one calf, or baby camel, at a time. The **gestation period**, or time between mating and birth, is 13 to 14 months. A cow that mates in January will give birth to her calf in February or March of the following year. When a cow is ready to give birth, she finds a sheltered place where she and her baby won't be disturbed.

Newborn camels have long, knobby legs, frizzy hair, and tiny humps. They measure a bit over 3.3 feet (1 m) at the shoulder and weigh about 73 pounds (33 kg). A wild Bactrian calf will try to stand up almost as soon as it's born. Within half an hour, the calf can walk a little bit.

Right: A mother nuzzles her young calf.
Below: Camels usually give birth to just one calf at a time.

It will look for its mother's udder, the gland that releases milk. By the next day, it can walk alongside its mother as she grazes. Every hour or two the calf nurses, or takes a drink of its mother's rich milk.

After about 3 weeks, mother and calf join a group of other cows and youngsters. While the mothers graze, the calves nurse, explore their surroundings, and chase one another. If a calf gets separated from its mother, another mother camel will let it nurse from her udder. The calf will nurse for more than a year.

It also starts eating plants at a few months old.

The first year is a dangerous time for calves. The desert is very hard on young camels. Calves must travel as far as the adults, but calves aren't as strong and don't have as much fat to provide energy. Many young camels die on the trail to distant oases.

If a calf survives, it continues to roam with its mother and other camels. When the calf is nearly a year old, its mother will be ready to breed again.

Camel calves nurse from their mothers for about a year.

Camels munch plants that brush their knees and plants that loom high above them.

She joins a harem and mates with a bull. She still cares for her 1-year-old calf. The calf will stay with her until she gives birth to the next calf the following year. By then, her 2-year-old youngster can take care of itself.

A young female usually stays near her mother and joins the same harem as her mother. A young male joins a group of other young bulls. They all continue to trek through the desert, eat, and grow. When camels are about 5 years old, they mate for the first time and have offspring of their own.

Bulls breed every year, as long as they can fight off rival males. Cows breed every other year until they die. Wild Bactrian camels live 20 to 30 years. Domesticated camels of both species may reach 50 years of age.

THE SHIP
OF THE DESERT

FOR THOUSANDS OF YEARS, DOMESTICATED CAMELS HAVE been important to humans. Camels have provided food and clothing, pulled plows, and carried cargo. They were so important to early travelers that people gave them the nickname ships of the desert.

Some camels made long-distance journeys. Dromedaries carried salt, gold, and cloth across the deserts of North Africa and the Middle East. Bactrian camels carried silk, spices, and gems across Asia. They traveled on a series of trails called the Silk Road. Between 100 B.C. and A.D. 1500, this route was the only way to travel from Europe to Asia. People traveled in large groups called caravans, with hundreds and sometimes thousands of camels.

For people on the early trade routes, camels were the only way to travel. Most trails were too rough and rocky for carts. Horses and donkeys needed too much food and water. They couldn't carry half as much weight as a camel could. A camel could carry more than 600 pounds (272 kg) of cinnamon or silk and never miss a step.

Camels also made shorter journeys. They lived with people called **nomads** (NOH-mads). Nomads are people with no permanent homes. Like camels, nomads of earlier centuries moved from oasis to oasis. Camels carried the people's belongings in baskets or sacks strapped around their humps. They also carried trade goods to be sold in towns at the edge of the desert.

Like ships crossing an ocean, camels cross vast deserts with their cargoes of people and supplies.

This man rides a Bactrian camel easily, settling in the space between the humps. Riding a camel can actually cause motion sickness. Camels move both legs on the same side at the same time, which makes them sway back and forth as they walk.

People usually walked alongside their camels. But sometimes people rode on camels. Bactrian camels are easy to ride, because the space between the two humps makes a secure seat. Dromedaries are not so easy to ride. So people invented different kinds of saddles for dromedaries. Some saddles rested on the front of the hump, some sat behind the hump, and some sat high on top of the hump.

When people needed meat or leather, they killed a camel. Camels also gave people milk. Every spring, camels shed their woolly coats. People either collected the fallen wool or cut it off before it was shed. In many nomadic cultures, people's survival depended on camels.

In many Middle Eastern lands, a family's wealth was measured not in gold or land but in camels.

While camped at an oasis, nomads let their camels loose to find food on their own. After the camels ate, they returned to camp to get water. The camels were not allowed to mate on their own, though. Their owners bred only those camels that had valuable traits, such as thick wool, large amounts of milk, or great strength. People sometimes mated dromedaries with Bactrian camels. This way, they created **hybrids** (mixed breeds) that were bigger and stronger than either parent species. Hybrid camels have one long hump with a dent in the middle.

The camel on the right is in the process of shedding its coat. One camel sheds about 11 pounds (5 kg) of soft, warm wool every spring. The camel on the left has fallen humps. It needs to store up on food.

A rancher in Australia chases a feral dromedary.

For centuries, people continued to use camels to carry riders and heavy loads. Between 1866 and 1900, Europeans brought thousands of dromedaries to Australia. The camels worked on expeditions where workers made maps, strung telegraph lines, and laid railroad tracks across Australia. Camels pulled carts and buggies. Police in Australia even patrolled on camelback until 1949. But eventually, machines took over the camels' jobs. By the mid-1900s, railroads and highways connected far-flung towns in Australia. Camels were no longer needed. People killed thousands of them. Thousands more were set loose in the desert, where they survived and had calves. In modern times, Australia is home to nearly 300,000 feral dromedaries.

With modern ships, roads, cars, and airplanes, people no longer need camels to carry trade goods across deserts and

In the 1850s, the U.S. Army imported about 120 camels, mostly dromedaries, to the American Southwest. The camels carried equipment on an expedition to survey, or map, the region. The camels did their job well, but the army had not brought along any skilled camel herders. The officers in charge of the camels didn't know how to care for them. They didn't even know that camels need to drink eventually. Without enough water, many camels died. When the Civil War started in 1861, the army ended its camel project. It turned the camels loose in the desert. They lived for a while on their own and even had offspring. But by the early 1900s, they had all died.

continents. Most people in North Africa and the Middle East live in towns and cities. Few of them are nomads. If they need to cross the desert, they take airplanes.

Throughout the Middle East, camels have less work to do than they once did. One of their biggest jobs is to give rides to tourists. Another job for modern dromedaries is racing. Camel racing is a popular sport in the Middle East.

In central Asia, the Silk Road is gone. But some rural people there still depend on domesticated Bactrian camels. They drink camels' milk and make it into cheese and yogurt. They harvest camels' woolly hair and use it to make blankets and coats. They also sell the wool to outsiders who value the soft, warm fiber.

In some parts of Australia, feral dromedaries have become pests. They devour some plants and trample others. They tear down fences and break pipes and water tanks. In other parts of the country, ranchers round up feral camels like cattle. The ranchers slaughter the camels for their meat. So far, camel meat is not very popular in Australia. If it becomes more popular, dromedaries could become important in Australia, just as they have been in the Middle East for centuries. This change could be a new chapter in the dromedary's long journey.

WHY BE WILD?

IF YOU WERE TO FLY OVER THE GOBI DESERT IN MONGOLIA and China, you might look for hours and never see a camel. Wild Bactrian camels are very afraid of humans. They run or hide as soon as they hear an engine or smell people approaching. Feral dromedaries in Australia are not as timid, but they can be just as hard to spot. Their tan coloring blends in with their desert surroundings. If they hold still, they can be almost impossible to see.

Despite these difficulties, biologists have found ways to study wild camels. They watch the camels through high-powered binoculars or from low-flying planes. Biologists have captured a few wild camels, fitted them with special collars, and then released them back into the wild. The collars send out signals, so biologists can track the camels

Domesticated camels have thrived in their partnership with humans. Their human keepers have fed them, bred them, and taken them to new lands. But wild camels have not been so successful. Wild dromedaries have been extinct for more than 2,000 years. As for wild Bactrian camels, fewer than 4,000 remain. They face an uncertain future. In fact, they are in danger of dying out completely.

Wild Bactrian camels once roamed across much of Asia. They lived from the Caspian Sea in western Russia to the Yellow River in China, and from Russia's Lake Baikal in the north to Tibet in the south. In modern times, they live in a tiny portion of their earlier range. They face tougher challenges than ever before.

When people domesticate animals, they breed them to become more valuable to humans. The animals lose traits that their wild ancestors once had. For instance, domesticated Bactrian camels may produce more hair or milk, run faster, or carry heavier loads than their wild relatives. But they cannot survive in harsh conditions as well as wild camels can. They don't find their way through the wilderness as well. They often have trouble finding food and water.

Biologists draw blood from a wild Bactrian camel in Mongolia to learn more about its health and how its body works. The testing will also help scientists learn about the differences between wild and domestic Bactrian camels.

Over the past 20 years, their desert homes have become warmer and drier. One-fourth of their oases have dried up. Camels must travel longer between drinks, and they don't always make it. Not strong enough to follow their mothers between distant oases, many camel calves die along the trails.

Humans have hurt camels in many ways. Thousands of people, working at oil wells, iron mines, and gold mines, have crowded the camels out. Highways and railroad tracks have split up their territory. The camels can't travel from one area to another to reach food or to mate with one another. Every year, people shoot many Bactrian camels for their meat or for sport. Even camels that manage to avoid the hunters still suffer. They will not go to oases if people are nearby. They must walk farther to reach other oases.

Some parts of the desert go for years without any rain at all. When that happens, water holes dry up, the ground bakes, and plants wither and die. Camels might die too.

A large herd of wild Bactrian camels in central Asia

For 40 years in the late 1900s, people tested nuclear bombs north of the Altun Mountains in China. This region is a Bactrian camel habitat. Nuclear explosions release deadly radiation into the air, water, and soil. Nobody knows what harm this radiation did to the camels, the plants they eat, and the water they drink.

Some people ask: why should we worry about wild camels? The answer is that wild camels are an essential part of their desert homes. Through their long treks, they link distant parts of the desert. They eat plants that other animals don't eat. When they die, their bodies provide food for animals called **scavengers**. These animals include wolves and vultures. Camels also help spread seeds from one place to another. Camels eat plants, including plant seeds. Later, the seeds end up in new places inside camels' dung.

To understand the differences among domesticated animals, feral animals, and their wild relatives, look at dogs and wolves. Dogs are the domesticated descendants of wild wolves. Dogs and wolves are alike in some ways, but they are very different in others. Even feral dogs, which run wild and no longer live with humans, are very different from wolves.

One wild Bacterian cow that was tracked by biologists traveled across more than 6,500 square miles (16,835 sq. km) in just one year.

As they gather food and water over long distances, wild camels contribute to their desert **ecosystem**. This is the network of living and nonliving things—such as plants, animals, soil, water, and air—that need one another to survive. Wild camels are a key part of their ecosystem. They can teach us a lot, if we will give them room to roam and a chance to survive.

China and Mongolia have established wildlife preserves to help protect camels and other animals. These preserves include the Arjin Mountain Nature Reserve in China and the Great Gobi Strictly Protected Area in Mongolia. In the preserves, hunting, building, and other human activities are not allowed. Biologists working at the preserves study camels and learn how to help them survive.

Wild Bactrian camels are on the World Conservation Union's list of critically endangered animals. Endangered animals are those that are likely to become extinct. In just 20 years, the number of wild Bactrian camels in Mongolia has dropped by half. Wild Bactrian camels are even rarer than giant pandas.

We will never know what we lost when wild dromedaries became extinct. Modern people know much more about wild Bactrian camels—enough to know that we will lose something very special if they disappear forever.

GLOSSARY

Bactrian camels: two-humped camels that live in central Asia. Their scientific name is *Camelus bactrianus.*

calluses: thick, tough patches of skin

camelids: Members of the camel family, which include camels, llamas, alpacas, vicuñas, and guanacos

Camelidae: the scientific name for the camel family

cud: a wad of food that has been swallowed at least once and then vomited up to be chewed again

deserts: areas that receive very little rainfall. Deserts are usually very hot in summer.

domesticated: bred and adapted for human use

dromedaries: one-humped camels native to the Middle East and northern Africa. Their scientific name is *Camelus dromedarius.* They are also called Arabian camels.

ecosystem: a network of living and nonliving things that share an environment

extinct: no longer existing. When every member of a plant or animal species has died out, that species is extinct.

feral: domesticated but living in the wild

gestation period: the time between when an animal mates and when it gives birth

habitat: the natural home of a plant or animal

harem: group of female camels gathered by a male camel during the breeding season

herbivores: animals that feed on plants

hybrids: animals or plants whose parents were of different species

musth: a condition a male camel enters when he is ready to mate

nomads: people with no permanent homes. Nomads often travel from place to place searching for food, water, or jobs.

oases: places in the desert where underground water comes close to the surface, allowing plants to grow

scavengers: animals that eat the bodies of animals they did not kill

species: a particular kind of animal or plant

SELECTED BIBLIOGRAPHY

Budiansky, Stephen. *The Covenant of the Wild: Why Animals Chose Domestication*. New York: William Morrow and Company, 1992.

Bulliet, Richard W. *The Camel and the Wheel*. New York: Columbia University Press Morningside Edition, 1990.

Gauthier-Pilters, Hilde, and Anne Innis Dagg. *The Camel: Its Evolution, Ecology, Behavior, and Relationship to Man*. Chicago: University of Chicago Press, 1981.

Reading, Richard P., Dulamtserengiin Enkhbileg, and Tuvdendorjiin Galbaatar, eds. *Ecology and Conservation of Wild Bactrian Camels*. Denver: Denver Zoological Foundation Series in Conservation Biology, 2002.

Schmidt-Nielsen, Knut. *Desert Animals: Physiological Problems of Heat and Water*. Oxford: Clarendon Press, 1964.

———*The Camel's Nose: Memoirs of a Curious Scientist*. Washington, DC: Island Press, 1998.

Sowell, John. *Desert Ecology*. Salt Lake City: University of Utah Press, 2001.

Young, J. Z. *The Life of Vertebrates*. 2nd ed. New York: Oxford University Press, 1962.

WEBSITES

ArabNet. "The A-Z of Camels."
    http://www.arab.net/camels/welcome.html
    Site visitors will find good basic information about domesticated dromedaries in the
    Middle East.
Oakland Zoo. "Dromedary (Arabian) Camel."
    http://www.oaklandzoo.org/meet_the_animals/dromedary-(arabian)-camel
    Visitors to this site will find general introductory material on dromedary camels, including
    their humps and their relationship with humans.
San Diego Zoo. "Mammals: Camel."
    http://www.sandiegozoo.org/animalbytes/t-camel.html
    This colorful Web page offers loads of information on camels, including video footage.

FURTHER READING

Barnes, Julia. *Camels and Llamas at Work*. Milwaukee: Gareth Stevens Publishing, 2006.

Camels. Milwaukee: Gareth Stevens Publishing, 2004.

Wexo, John Bonnett. *The Camel Family*. Poway, CA: Wildlife Education, 2001.

INDEX

ABOUT THE AUTHOR

Cherie Winner is a science writer for *Washington State Magazine*. She also writes books. Her published titles include *Cryobiology, Life in the Tundra, Life on the Edge, Salamanders, Trout,* and *Woodpeckers*. Winner holds a Ph.D. in zoology from Ohio State University. She lives in Pullman, Washington.

PHOTO ACKNOWLEDGMENTS

The images in this book are used with permission of: © Theo Allofs/Photonica/Getty Images, all backgrounds, pp. 1, 5, 10, 16, 22 (both); 26, 32, 38, 44, 45, 46, 47, 48; © Richard Reading, pp. 2-3, 7, 23 (bottom), 26, 28, 29 (top), 31, 34, 39, 41, 42; © Michele Burgess, pp. 4, 13 (bottom); © James P. Rowan, pp. 5, 11 (both), 13 (top right), 20; © Karlene Schwartz, pp. 6 (both), 12 (both), 14 (top); © Laura Westlund/Independent Picture Service, p. 8; © Cory Langley, pp. 9, 16, 18 (bottom), 40; © Kenneth W. Fink/Root Resources, pp. 10, 15, 18 (top), 23 (top); © Science VU/D.C.H. Plowes/Visuals Unlimited, p. 13 (top left); © Claudia Adams/Root Resources, p. 14 (bottom); © Kjell Sandved/Visuals Unlimited, p. 17 (top); © Henry Ausloos/Peter Arnold, Inc., p. 17 (bottom); © Dr. Rudolf G. Arndt/Visuals Unlimited, p. 19; © Doug Allan/naturepl.com, p. 24; PhotoDisc Royalty Free by Getty Images, p. 25; AP Photo/Hassene Dridi, p. 27; © Tiziana and Gianni Baldizzone/CORBIS, p. 29 (bottom); © Hanne & Jens Eriksen/naturepl.com, pp. 30, 45; © Ruth Welty/Root Resources, p. 32; © Pete Oxford/naturepl.com, p. 33; © Gertrud & Helmet Denzau/naturepl.com, p. 35; AP Photo/Central Australian Camel Industry Association, p. 36; © Ken Lucas/Visuals Unlimited, p. 38.

Front Cover: © Ken Lucas/Visuals Unlimited.

Back Cover: © Theo Allofs/Photonica/Getty Images.